Pebble®
Plus

I Want a Pet
I Want a Cat

by Kimberly M. Hutmacher

Consulting Editor: Gail Saunders-Smith, PhD

Consultant: Jennifer Zablotny, DVM
Member, American Veterinary Medical Association

CAPSTONE PRESS
a capstone imprint

Pebble Plus is published by Capstone Press,
1710 Roe Crest Drive, North Mankato, Minnesota 56003.
www.capstonepub.com

 Books published by Capstone Press are manufactured with paper
containing at least 10 percent post-consumer waste.

Library of Congress Cataloging-in-Publication Data
Hutmacher, Kimberly.
  I want a cat / by Kimberly M. Hutmacher.
    p. cm.—(Pebble plus. I want a pet)
  Includes bibliographical references and index.
  Summary: "Simple text and full-color photographs describe the responsibilities involved in caring for and choosing a
cat as a pet"—Provided by publisher.
  ISBN 978-1-4296-7596-3 (library binding)
  1. Cats—Juvenile literature. I. Title.
  SF445.7.H88 2012
  636.8—dc23   2011021649

Editorial Credits
Erika L. Shores, editor; Bobbie Nuytten, designer; Sarah Schuette, photo stylist; Marcy Morin, studio scheduler;
    Kathy McColley, production specialist

Photo Credits
All photographs by Capstone Studio/Karon Dubke, except Shutterstock: Eric Gevaert, design element

Note to Parents and Teachers

The I Want a Pet series supports common core state standards for English language arts related
to reading informational text. This book describes and illustrates cat ownership. The images
support early readers in understanding the text. The repetition of words and phrases helps early
readers learn new words. This book also introduces early readers to subject-specific vocabulary
words, which are defined in the Glossary section. Early readers may need assistance to read
some words and to use the Table of Contents, Glossary, Read More, Internet Sites, and Index
sections of the book.

Printed in the United States of America in North Mankato, Minnesota.
102011   006405CGS12

Table of Contents

Cats Are for Me

Would you love the sweet purr

of a cat sitting on your lap?

What are the responsibilities

of owning a cat? Let's find out.

My Responsibilities

Cats need lots of attention. You'll play with your cat and talk to it. You'll care for your pet every day.

Each day you'll give your cat food and water. Kittens eat smaller amounts than adults. But kittens need to eat more often.

Your cat will use a litter box.

You'll have to scoop out

poop daily. Once a week,

you'll replace the litter.

Most cats won't use a dirty box.

A curious cat needs

to be taught what is off limits.

You'll want it to use

a scratching post rather

than scratch on furniture.

Choosing the *Purrfect Cat*

Are you ready for a pet cat?
What kind of cat is right
for your family? Will it be
a calm, lovable adult,
or a playful, curious kitten?

Cats and kittens in animal shelters
need good homes. Do you want
a certain cat breed?
Find a breeder who sells
that kind of cat.

Now it's time to buy a bed,
a litter box, food, bowls,
and toys. Don't forget a brush
to care for your cat's fur.

Take your cat to the veterinarian for a checkup and vaccinations. Healthy cats can live 15 years or longer. Enjoy each day with your furry friend!

Glossary

animal shelter—a safe place where lost or homeless pets can stay

breed—a certain kind of animal within an animal group

breeder—a person who raises animals to sell

healthy—fit and well, not sick

litter box—a container indoors for a cat to go to the bathroom; owners must clean litter boxes every day

vaccination—a shot of medicine to prevent disease

veterinarian—a doctor who treats sick or injured animals; veterinarians also help animals stay healthy

Read More

Armentrout, David. *Kitty Care.* Let's Talk about Pets. Vero Beach, Fla.: Rourke Pub., 2011.

Bearce, Stephanie. *Care for a Kitten.* How to Convince Your Parents You Can. Hockessin, Del.: Mitchell Lane, 2010.

Ganeri, Anita. *Cats.* A Pet's Life. Chicago: Heinemann Library, 2009.

Internet Sites

FactHound offers a safe, fun way to find Internet sites related to this book. All of the sites on FactHound have been researched by our staff.

Here's all you do:

Visit *www.facthound.com*

Type in this code: 9781429675963

Super-cool stuff! Check out projects, games and lots more at **www.capstonekids.com**

Index

Word Count: 222
Grade: 1
Early-Intervention Level: 15